Scary Hair

Written by Jill Eggleton
Illustrated by Rita Parkinson

Scarecrow was sad.

"Look at me.
I have a hat," he said.

"I have a nose
and I have a mouth.

But I have no hair!"

"Poor Scarecrow,"
said the farmer.

"I will find your hair."

The farmer put a notice
in the newspaper.

Lost
Scarecrow's Hair
Reward $100.00
Phone: The Farmer
19 218 5463

LOST & FOUND

Lost
Scarecrow's Hair
Reward $100.00
Phone: The Farmer
19 218 5463

"We will look
for Scarecrow's hair,"
said the people.

They looked in holes.
"The hair is not here,"
they said.

They looked under plants.
"The hair is not here,"
they said.

They looked in the trees.
"Here is Scarecrow's hair!"
they said.

"Good!" said Scarecrow.
"I have hair.
But . . . I have no shoes!"

An Advertisement

▰▰ Guide Notes

Title: Scarecrow's Hair
Stage: Early (1) – Red

Genre: Fiction
Approach: Guided Reading
Processes: Thinking Critically, Exploring Language, Processing Information
Written and Visual Focus: Advertisement
Word Count: 97

THINKING CRITICALLY
(sample questions)
- What do you think this story could be about?
- What do you know about scarecrows?
- Why do people have scarecrows?
- Look at page 2. Why do you think the scarecrow looks sad?
- Look at page 8. Where do you think the farmer could be?
- What do you think this is on page 9? (advertisement)
- Look at page 12. Where do you think the scarecrow's hair could be?
- Look at page 14. What do you think the scarecrow could be thinking now?

EXPLORING LANGUAGE

Terminology
Title, cover, illustrations, author, illustrator

Vocabulary
Interest words: scarecrow, reward, notice, newspaper
High-frequency words: have, will, looked, they
Positional words: under, in
Compound words: newspaper, scarecrow

Print Conventions
Capital letter for sentence beginnings and name (**S**carecrow), full stops,
exclamation marks, quotation marks, commas, ellipsis